75 *fabulous* Fabric Crafts

Easy *Projects*
with **makings**™
Craft Fabrics

Landauer Books

Table of *contents*

Crafting with fabric is my all-time favorite thing to do... and finding that special fabric has never been so convenient! More than simple fat quarters, MAKINGS™ Craft Fabrics offer a broad assortment of fashionable, coordinated styles in a variety of great colors.

With the ideas and inspiration found in **75 Fabulous Fabric Crafts** *and your favorite MAKINGS™ prints, you can create stunning projects for decorating your home, giving as gifts and wearing with pride.*

Craft one of these easy, no-sew projects today. The possibilities are endless!

Deni

Deni Thompson
MAKINGS™
Craft Project Manager

PS—If you are a beginner to fabric crafting or just need a few helpful hints, be sure to check out the Crafting with Fabric section on pages 45-47.

Home Decorating

Wearables for All Ages

Kid Gear

Celebrate! Special Days

Crafting with Fabrics

What is a **craft fabric?**

Most fabric is sold by the yard, but many projects require smaller portions of fabric. Shops thus began selling craft fabrics or "fat quarters"— pieces of fabric which are half a yard cut in half, measuring 18" × 22". Crafts and fabric stores offer many patterns, colors and designs to choose from, and you can purchase craft fabrics individually or in coordinated bundles.

HOME
decorating

There's nothing like a touch of your favorite
fabric to turn any room in your home into
an expression of your personal style.
Pick out a craft fabric or two, check out
these simple crafts and start decorating!

apples
in the kitchen

RECIPE BOX AND CARDS SUPPLIES

Walnut Hollow® wood box
1 MAKINGS™ craft fabric
each: red check and
green swirls
Plaid® Folk Art Craft
Paints, yellow and
brown
Aleene's® Original "Tacky
Glue"™
Wood apple shape
Plaid® Mod Podge®, matte
Therm O Web HeatnBond
Lite iron-on adhesive
Liquitex® acrylic gesso
paint, white
Sandpaper
Rub-on letters
Index cards, 4" × 6"
Apple buttons

RECIPE BOX AND CARDS INSTRUCTIONS

1. Sand wood box and apple shape.
2. Paint wood box with gesso paint. Let dry.
3. Trace and cut out an apple shape from the HeatnBond and red-check fabric. Fuse both to the wood apple shape.
4. Trace and cut a leaf shape from the green swirls fabric and HeatnBond. Fuse both to the apple shape.
5. Paint apple stem brown.
6. Coat completed apple shape with Mod Podge. Let dry.
7. Glue apple shape to the box front with the fabric glue.
8. Tie a green-swirls print fabric strip bow around knob on box top for trim.
9. Use rub-on letters to add "Recipes" to apple front
10. For cards, trim index cards to fit inside the box. Glue strips of red-check fabric along the top edge of each card. Make card dividers from manila file folders and cover with coordinating fabric. Trim with apple buttons.

TRAY AND COASTERS SUPPLIES

Walnut Hollow® serving tray, 15" × 11" × 2¼"

1 MAKINGS™ craft fabric each: blue check/red flowers, green swirls and red check

Plaid® Folk Art Acrylic Paints, red and brown

Plaid® Mod Podge®, matte

Liquitex® gesso paint, white

Sandpaper

Spray acrylic varnish

10 four-inch wood apple shapes, ⅛" thick

Therm O Web HeatnBond Lite iron-on adhesive

Felt, red

Rickrack ribbon, yellow

TRAY AND COASTERS INSTRUCTIONS

1. Sand and paint tray with gesso paint. Let dry. Paint tray and six apple shapes red. Let dry.
2. Paint all apple stems brown. Let dry.
3. Apply HeatnBond to all fabric. Trace and cut out leaf shapes using the green swirls fabric. Glue to six apple shapes with Mod Podge. Cut six small squares from red-check fabric and apply to the apple shapes with Mod Podge to add a "blush" to the apples.
4. Cut the blue-check fabric to fit the tray bottom. Apply fabric to the tray with Mod Podge. Let dry. Glue six painted apple shapes atop the blue fabric in the bottom of the tray with Mod Podge. Coat apples and fabric in tray with Mod Podge.
5. For coasters, cover the remaining four apple shapes with the red-check fabric and Mod Podge. Cut felt apple shapes and glue to the back of each coaster. Bundle the set of four coasters with rickrack ribbon.

NAPKINS SUPPLIES

Makes 2 napkins and 2 ties

2 MAKINGS™ craft fabrics each: blue-check/ red flowers and yellow check

1 MAKINGS™ craft fabric: red check

DMC® #5 pearl cotton thread, red

2 apple buttons

Wavy-edged scissors or rotary cutter

NAPKINS INSTRUCTIONS

1. Match wrong sides of the yellow check and blue check with red flowers fabrics together.
2. Trim edges with wavy-edged scissors.
3. With red pearl cotton, use a running stitch ¾" from outside edge to sew pieces together.
4. Cut two 3-inch circles from the blue-check fabric and make two yo-yos. See page 41 for complete yo-yo instructions. Add a yo-yo and apple button to each napkin.
5. Cut six 1" × 7" strips of bias-cut red-check fabric. Braid three red-check strips together for each napkin. Tie around folded napkin for ring.

DISH TOWELS SUPPLIES

3 tea towels, 18" × 24"
4 MAKINGS™ craft
fabrics:
For red towel—blue
check with red flowers
For yellow towel—red
check and green swirls
For red/white towel—
apple print
Therm O Web HeatnBond
Lite iron-on adhesive
DMC® #5 pearl cotton
thread, red and green
Medium-size rickrack
ribbon, red and yellow
Apple buttons

DISH TOWELS INSTRUCTIONS

1. For the red towel, apply HeatnBond to the blue-check and red flowers fabric. Measure and cut a 3-inch-wide band of fabric with a wavy-edged rotary cutter. Fuse the fabric band to the towel and stitch rickrack ribbon along the top and bottom edge with red pearl cotton.

2. For the yellow towel, trim with a 1-inch-wide wavy-edge green swirl fabric band and yellow rickrack ribbon. Add three red-checked yo-yos made from 3-inch-diameter circles. See page 41 for complete yo-yo instructions. Sew on apple buttons. Cut 2 leaf shapes from the green swirls fabric and fuse to the towel. Outline the leaf shapes with a button hole stitch in green floss.

3. For the red/white towel, cut out and fuse three apples from the apple print fabric along edge of towel. Outline the apples with a button hole stitch with red floss. Add rickrack ribbon with pearl cotton thread.

quick-pick accessories

TRIVET SUPPLIES

Glass saucer-style
candleholder
2 MAKINGS™ craft
fabrics: apple print
1 Makings™ craft fabric:
red check
Plaid® Mod Podge®, matte
Felt, red (to cover top
of candle holder)
Aleene's® Thick Designer
"Tacky Glue"™

TRIVET INSTRUCTIONS

1. Measure the circumference of the candleholder base and cut a piece of the apple print to match. Apply Mod Podge to the fabric piece and secure it to the inside of the base.

2. Cut several 1-inch-wide bias strips from the apple print and the red-check fabric. Tie strips together to form longer strips of each fabric. Braid two apple print strips with one red-check strip.

3. Measure and cut a circle of red felt to cover the top of the candleholder. Glue felt to the glass top.

4. Cover the felt with fabric glue. Starting at the center, coil the braided fabric strip and press firmly to secure. Continue coiling until the top is completely covered.

tribal
desk set

TRUNK SUPPLIES

Wooden trunk
1 MAKINGS™ craft fabric
  each of two
  coordinating designs
Hirschberg cording and
  tassel, black
Plaid® Mod Podge®, matte
Plasticote® spray crackle,
  gold and black
Hot-glue gun and glue
  sticks

DESK MAT SUPPLIES

Desk calendar mat
  (available at office
  supply stores)
1 MAKINGS™ craft fabric
Hirschberg gimp trim
Plaid® Mod Podge®, matte
Hot-glue gun and glue
  sticks

PENCIL CUP
SUPPLIES

1 MAKINGS™ craft fabric
  each of two
  coordinating designs
Plaid® Mod Podge®, matte
Mrs. Glue™ fabric glue
Flower pot, 4-inch
  diameter
Hirschberg cording
Hirschberg tassel
Delta Ceramcoat® acrylic
  paint, black

TRUNK INSTRUCTIONS

1. Spray box (inside and out) with Plasticote's spray crackle according to package directions. Let dry.
2. Trace patterns for box exterior insets and cut fabric to fit.
3. Use Mod Podge to attach fabric onto each inset. Let dry.
4. Glue cording around fabric edges with hot glue. Trim excess.
5. Glue tassel under the box closure.

DESK MAT INSTRUCTIONS

1. Measure and cut fabric strips to cover sides of desk mat, allowing for an additional 3 inches to wrap around the back of the mat.
2. Use Mod Podge to adhere fabric onto the front of the mat, keeping straight any pattern on the fabric.
3. Fold fabric around to the mat back and secure corners tightly with hot glue. Decoupage fabric onto the back.
4. Glue trim in place, referring to the photograph for placement.

PENCIL CUP INSTRUCTIONS

1. Measure circumference of flower pot base and top edge.
2. Paint inside of pot.
3. Cut strips of desired fabric to fit each section.
4. Use Mod Podge to adhere fabrics onto the pot.
5. Glue cording onto pot with fabric glue.
6. Glue tassel in place.

toile
style at work

LAMP SUPPLIES
Lamp base and fabric shade
1 MAKINGS™ craft fabric: black toile
1 pkg. Hirschberg fringe trim and matching tassel, black/white
Aleene's® Thick Designer "Tacky Glue"™
Therm O Web PeelnStick™ ¼"-wide double-sided adhesive
Spray paint, black
Straight pins
Tape measure

LAMP INSTRUCTIONS
1. Spray-paint lamp base and shade. Let dry.
2. To determine the length of the fabric bias tape, measure around the top and bottom of the shade.
3. Fold fabric in half diagonally and press fold. Cut on the fold.
4. Measure 2 inches from a diagonal edge, then cut a 2-inch-wide bias strip.
5. Continue to cut 2-inch–wide bias strips to equal the lengths determined in Step 2.
6. Fold and press each strip in half lengthwise. Fold outer edges in to meet at the center fold. Fold in half again and press to make each strip.
7. Place double-sided adhesive along the shade top and bottom edges of both the outside and inside surfaces, keeping it straight and even.
8. Open the bias strip to place the center fold on the edge of the shade. Starting at the shade seam, press the bias strip onto the adhesive on the outside of the shade, again keeping the edge straight. Fold the bias strip to the inside of the shade top and bottom and press onto the adhesive.
9. Starting again at the shade seam, glue fringe trim on inside bottom of shade with Aleene's Thick Designer "Tacky Glue." Secure the trim while gluing by barely poking straight pins into the shade edge. Remove pins when glue is dry.
10. Add tassel to lamp base as shown.

CLOCK SUPPLIES

Walnut Hollow® clock plaque 7" × 7" and ¾" deep
Walnut Hollow® clock works to fit ¾" plaque
Spray paint, black
Walnut Hollow® clock numbers (1" numbers shown, painted black)
1 MAKINGS™ craft fabric: black toile
Plaid® Mod Podge®, matte
Awl
Painter's tape
1 yard of Hirschberg Chinese braid, black
Mrs. Glue™ fabric glue

CLOCK INSTRUCTIONS

1. Cut fabric to 9" × 9".
2. Center fabric square over the front of clock plaque and smoothly brush on Mod Podge with a foam paintbrush, coating the fabric completely. Fold fabric edges over to the clock back, making smooth corners and smooth fabric edges. Prop the clock on a solid surface to let dry.
3. When dry, turn plaque face down and cover fabric edges with painter's tape. Spray back of plaque with spray paint and, if necessary, paint the clock hands and numbers. Let dry.
4. Poke hole in center of plaque, through the fabric, with the awl.
5. Following directions on the clock-works package, assemble clock.
6. Glue numbers onto the clock face.
7. Measure and then add Chinese braid around clock edge with fabric glue.

Work spaces don't have to be boring! Popular toiles can bring style into any office.

STOOL SUPPLIES

Wood stool
Delta Ceramcoat® paint, black
Delta Ceramcoat® satin varnish
1 MAKINGS™ craft fabric: black toile
1 pkg. Hirschberg fringe trim, black and white
Batting
Heavy-duty staple gun
Hammer
Upholstery tacks, black
Tape measure
Paintbrush

STOOL INSTRUCTIONS

1. Paint the legs and bottom of the stool. When dry, apply a coat of varnish.
2. Measure the length and width of the top of the stool.
3. Cut a piece of fabric 4 inches larger in length and width than the stool measurement, making sure the fabric design is straight.
4. Cut four pieces of batting the same size as the fabric.
5. Fold the fabric edges in 1 inch and press.
6. Lay fabric right side down on a flat surface. Center batting pieces on top of fabric and center the stool upside down on the batting. Pull fabric around to underside edge of the stool and tack with staple gun. Repeat on all sides.
7. Measure, then secure the fringe trim around the stool edge by pounding upholstery tacks around the edge evenly with a hammer.

...leopards and tigers and style, oh my!

FRAME SUPPLIES

1 MAKINGS™ craft fabric: leopard print
8" × 10" photo frame
Plaid® Mod Podge®, matte
Hirschberg Chinese braid, black
Hot-glue gun and glue sticks
4 Dress It Up® buttons, gold

FRAME INSTRUCTIONS

1. Place frame on the wrong side of the fabric. Trace around the frame, adding 2 inches to the length and width.
2. Use Mod Podge to adhere fabric onto the frame.
3. Glue braid onto frame, referring to the photograph for placement.
4. Glue buttons onto frame.

BOARD SUPPLIES

18" × 14" piece of ½"-thick foam core board
2 MAKINGS™ craft fabrics: tiger print
⅜"-wide satin ribbon
Hirschberg gimp trim
5 1-inch-diameter Dress It Up® buttons
24" of 24-gauge wire
Batting
Therm O Web HeatnBond iron-on adhesive
Hot-glue gun and glue sticks
Yarn needle

BOARD INSTRUCTIONS

1. Cut two pieces of batting the same size as the foam core. Place fabric right side down on a flat surface. Center batting pieces on the fabric and center the foam core on the batting. Pull fabric edges taut to the back of the foam core. Secure with hot glue.
2. Using the photo as a guide, cut ribbon and trim to fit diagonally across the bulletin board. Secure the ends with hot glue.
3. Use the yarn needle to pierce two holes through the board where each button is desired. Beginning at the board back, use wire to sew buttons on the front of the board. Cut and twist the wire after each button.
4. Apply HeatnBond to an 18" × 14" piece of fabric and fuse to the back of the board.
5. Glue gimp trim around outer edge of board with hot glue.

BASKET SUPPLIES

***Therm O Web HeatnBond
iron-on adhesive***

Picnic basket

***1 MAKINGS™ craft fabric
each: black vintage
with zinnias, yellow
flower/vine, green
swirls***

Batting

7" cardboard circle

***Hot-glue gun and glue
sticks***

Screwdriver

BASKET INSTRUCTIONS

1. Remove lid from picnic basket.
2. Measure and cut three pieces of batting the same size as the basket lid. Place black vintage print fabric right side down on a flat surface. Center and layer batting on the fabric. Center lid on the batting. Secure edges of fabric with hot glue.
3. Measure and cut a piece of fabric to cover the inside of the basket lid. Apply HeatnBond to the fabric and fuse to the inside surface of the lid, covering the black vintage print fabric edges.
4. Cut out a 9-inch circle of yellow print fabric and a 7-inch circle of batting.
5. Place batting, then fabric on 7-inch cardboard circle. Pull fabric edges around to the back of the cardboard circle and secure with hot glue.
6. To make a ruffle for the fabric circle, tear green swirls fabric into 3-inch strips. Sew short edges of strips together to make a large circle. Gather one edge. Glue ruffle to the edge on the back of the fabric circle. Glue the circle to the top center of the basket.

NAPKIN SUPPLIES

Makes 2 napkins

***1 MAKINGS™ craft
fabric: yellow flower/
vine print***

NAPKIN INSTRUCTIONS

1. Tear fabric in half to make two 9" × 11" napkins.
2. Remove threads one at a time from each edge of the fabric to fray to desired width.

vintage
picnic
basket set

*Vintage or
reproduction
fabrics
are not just
for quilting
anymore!*

FLORAL FRAME SUPPLIES

ProvoCraft Memory Frame, wood
1 MAKINGS™ craft fabric: floral print
Plaid® Mod Podge®, matte
⅜" ribbon

FLORAL FRAME INSTRUCTIONS

1. Measure and cut a 14½-inch square of fabric.
2. Apply Mod Podge to front and sides of the frame and then lay it face down and centered on the back side of the fabric.
3. Cut an X in the photo window, ending at each window corner. Pull the fabric triangles up and through the photo window to the back side of the frame. Secure with Mod Podge.
4. Wrap the outside edges of the frame by pulling the fabric back, folding the corners neatly. Secure with Mod Podge.
5. Measure, cut and glue ribbon around the outside edges of the frame and the inside of the photo window.
6. Use the cardboard photo back to crop and cut your photo for the frame.

VACATION MEMORY BOOK SUPPLIES

Walnut Hollow® Memory Album Cover
1 MAKINGS™ craft fabric: turquoise sprinkles print
Spray sizing
DecoArt® Staining/ Antiquing Medium
Delta Ceramcoat® acrylic paint, turquoise
DecoArt® gel stain, ebony
Plaid® Mod Podge®, matte
DecoArt® painter's pen
Assorted shells

VACATION MEMORY BOOK INSTRUCTIONS

1. Separate the front and back covers. Collect the posts and screws and set aside for reassembling.
2. For easier trimming, stiffen fabric by applying sizing and ironing.
3. Lay the front cover face down on the back side of the fabric and trace around it. Cut out the shape and test-fit it to the album cover.
4. Apply Mod Podge to the cover and place the fabric on the cover. Apply additional Mod Podge to the surface of the fabric.
5. Carefully cut the fabric around the hinges and poke the fabric through to the back side. Trim edges to fit.
6. Mix two parts staining medium with one part acrylic paint.
7. Spread paint mixture on the back cover and front spine and remove excess by wiping with a paper towel. Let dry.
8. For a more weathered look, wipe gel stain onto the wood on back cover and front spine. Let dry.
9. Print album title on the cover with a painter's pen. Add shell design.

GROOVY BOX SUPPLIES

Jewelry box, wood
1 MAKINGS™ craft fabric: VW beetle print
1 Makings™ craft fabric: black and rainbow stripes
Plaid® Mod Podge®, matte
Felt
Delta Ceramcoat® acrylic paint, black
Mrs. Glue™ fabric glue
Chenille cording, red
Flower button

GROOVY BOX INSTRUCTIONS

1. Remove hinge hardware from the jewelry box.
2. Measure the sides of the box bottom and cut a strip of fabric to fit.
3. Apply Mod Podge to the box bottom and place the fabric, aligning the top edges of the fabric to the box edges. Turn the fabric under to the bottom of the box, clipping the corners to fit.
4. Paint the top and insides of the box with acrylic paint. Let dry.
5. Cut out design motifs such as the cars and flowers from the second fabric. Apply them to the box as desired with Mod Podge. See the photograph for details.
6. Measure and cut a square of felt to fit the box bottom exterior. Glue with fabric glue.
7. Glue on chenille cording and button.

BUTTON JAR SUPPLIES

Glass jar with lid
1 MAKINGS™ craft fabric: patchwork hearts print
Poly-Fil™ batting
Rubber band
Rickrack ribbon
Assorted buttons
Hot-glue gun and glue sticks

BUTTON JAR INSTRUCTIONS

1. Measure the diameter of the jar lid, add 2 inches and cut a circle of fabric.
2. Roll batting or Poly-Fil into a fat pillow and place on the lid.
3. Center fabric circle over the batting and secure it to the jar lid with the rubber band. Tie a bow from ribbon or strip of fabric to cover the rubber band.
4. Measure the circumference of the jar, add ½ inch and cut rickrack to that length. Glue rickrack and assorted buttons to the jar with hot glue.

**Papier-maché box, metal
  tin, wooden crate**
**MAKINGS™ craft fabrics:
  coordinated colors and
  designs**
**Assorted ribbon, buttons,
  cording and jewels**
Plaid® Mod Podge®, matte
Mrs. Glue™ fabric glue
**Hot-glue gun and
  glue sticks**
**Magnetic letters (for
  metal use)**

CONTAINERS INSTRUCTIONS

1. Select the desired container and measure the sections you wish
   to cover with fabric.
2. If desired, paint any surfaces that will not be covered with fabric.
   Let dry.
3. Apply Mod Podge to the box, crate or tin surface and position
   the fabric, trimming or overlapping edges and wrapping them to
   the insides and back of the container.
4. Glue ribbon, buttons or jewels where desired with hot glue or
   fabric glue. Refer to the photograph on page 12 for ideas.
5. Get creative with finishing touches such as tying torn fabric
   strips to handles or adding jewels or cording. Personalization and
   labels can be added with hand-painted lettering, add-on letters or
   even magnetic letters on tin surfaces.

CAMP BINDER
SUPPLIES

5½" × 8½" 3-ring binder
**1 MAKINGS™ craft fabric
  each: yellow, orange
  and bug print**
Mrs. Glue™ fabric glue
**Delta Ceramcoat® acrylic
  paint, red**
¾" wood letters
Dress It Up® bug buttons

CAMP BINDER INSTRUCTIONS

1. Measure and cut two pieces of bug
   patterned fabric 6½" × 11½" each.
   Position fabric on the outside
   edges of the front and back of
   the album, allowing about ½-inch
   overlap per side to wrap to the
   inside. Glue in place.
2. Measure and cut the yellow fabric to 7½" × 11½".
   Center fabric on the album spine and glue.
   Overlap ¼ inch on the edge that meets the patterned fabric.
   Wrap the top and bottom to the inside of the album.
3. Cut two pieces of orange fabric measuring 7" × 9½" and 10½" × 9½".
   Glue the larger piece to the album inside front. Glue the smaller
   piece to the inside back. Turn under ¼ inch at the edges. Glue.
4. Paint wooden letters. Let dry.
5. Using wire cutter, cut spools off the bug buttons. Glue
   wooden letters and bug buttons to front of binder. See the
   photograph for details.

TRIP JOURNAL
SUPPLIES

**Paper Reflections®
  Memory Book, 6" × 8"**
**1 MAKINGS™ craft fabric
  each: inspirational
  words print, orange**
Mrs. Glue™ fabric glue
Vinyl letters

TRIP JOURNAL INSTRUCTIONS

1. Cut printed fabric to 6½" × 7½" to cover the front of the journal.
   Glue to journal front with fabric glue.
2. Cut the plain fabric to 6½" × 7½". Fray all edges the desired amount by
   using a straight pin to separate threads.
3. On the back of the frayed fabric, draw a diagonal line with a
   pencil from one corner to the opposite corner. Repeat with the
   remaining two corners. Next, draw a horizontal line parallel to the
   top of the fabric, about 1 inch from the edge. Where the line
   connects to each of the diagonal lines, draw a line down to the
   lower diagonal line. Then connect the bottom points, parallel to the
   top horizontal line. Cut out this inner rectangle. Center the plain
   fabric over the printed fabric and glue with fabric glue.
4. Add the title to the cover with vinyl letters.

wearables

for all ages

Make a fashion statement with a little imagination, a collection of fun craft fabrics and these easy-to-do projects. Create a unique item for yourself, or present family and friends with a memorable gift.

floral
fashion

EMBELLISHED VEST SUPPLIES

1 MAKINGS™ craft fabric: blue floral print

Therm O Web HeatnBond iron-on adhesive tape, ½"

2 skeins DMC® #5 pearl cotton thread

4 pkgs. Bead Heaven 6-mm crystal glass beads

EMBELLISHED VEST INSTRUCTIONS

1. Cut 1-inch-wide bias strips of fabric. Press raw edges to wrong side.
2. Use ½-inch-wide fusible tape to adhere bias fabric strips to edge of vest and pockets. Whipstitch over fabric with pearl cotton, adding a glass bead every half inch.

FLORAL HAT SUPPLIES

Hat
1 MAKINGS™ craft fabric
each: denim, pink
check, pink/blue
splatter print
Flower supply list for
corsage (see below)

FLORAL HAT INSTRUCTIONS

1. For hat band, cut bias strips of fabric 2-inches-wide and the length of the hat band from both the denim and pink-check craft fabrics. Press raw edges to wrong side creating 1-inch-wide finished strips.
2. Braid strips together and hand-stitch or glue to hat for a band.
3. Make flowers from the pattern on page 48 with the multicolor and pink-check fabrics, using artificial flowers for centers. Follow the instructions below.
4. Trace pattern onto fusing paper. Fuse to wrong side of fabric. Cut out. Add to flower center and secure with floral tape. Add leaves.
5. Use glue or hand-stitch flowers to hat.

CORSAGE SUPPLIES

1 MAKINGS™ craft fabric
each: blue floral print,
pink floral print,
blue check
4" felt circle
Pin back
Fibre Craft Panacea
Products #32-gauge
cloth-covered wire
Floral stem-wrap tape
Modern Romance Inc.
artificial leaves and
flowers, white stamens
Therm O Web HeatnBond
iron-on adhesive

CORSAGE INSTRUCTIONS

1. Apply HeatnBond to the desired fabric. Using the pattern on page 48, trace and cut out six heart shapes.
2. Trace and cut out a 3-inch circle. Remove HeatnBond paper backing from the circle.
3. Fold an 8-inch length of wire in half over a scrap of batting and twist to secure. With needle and thread, gather outer edge of fabric circle, slip over batting pulling thread tight. Knot thread.
4. Bend five white stamens in half and secure with the wire. Add stamens to the fabric center and wrap both wire pieces with floral tape.
5. Hand-pleat the bottom point of a fabric heart, insert it into flower center and wrap with floral tape to secure. Repeat with remaining hearts, adding petals around center to form flower. Continue wrapping wire stem with floral tape, adding leaves. Coil end of wire.
6. Make two flowers with fabric center and white stamens and one flower with artificial-flower center. Whip-stitch flowers to circle of felt and attach a pin back to the back with glue.

KITCHEN APRON SUPPLIES

Innovation Imagination Apron, 20" × 28"

1 MAKINGS™ craft fabric each: yellow check and apple print

5 apple buttons

DMC #5 pearl cotton thread, red

Medium-size rickrack ribbon, red

Therm O Web HeatnBond iron-on adhesive

aprons as art

GARDEN APRON AND GLOVES SUPPLIES

Innovation Imagination Creation Pocketfulls Apron, 19½" × 29"

1 MAKINGS™ craft fabric each: floral print, green/yellow wave stripe, orange/yellow wave stripe

Therm O Web HeatnBond Lite iron-on adhesive

Dress It Up® flower buttons

Fusible flower appliqués

Garden gloves

KITCHEN APRON INSTRUCTIONS

1. Cut the yellow check fabric on the bias 3 inches wide and twice the width of the apron at the bib long. Press the raw lengthwise sides to wrong side, meeting at the center. Turn under raw short ends.
2. Make five box pleats, evenly spaced, across the yellow-check fabric to the finished width of apron bib. Fuse pleats in place.
3. Place the pleated fabric strip to apron top and with a running stitch, sew in place with rickrack ribbon. Sew apple buttons onto pleats .
4. For the pockets, cut two 6½″ x 14″ rectangles from the apple fabric.
5. Press raw edges under half an inch along the long sides. Press fabric in half cross wise with wrong sides facing. Press points at bottom edge of pockets.
6. Stitch ribbon to the top of each pocket. Stitch pockets to apron.

GARDEN APRON AND GLOVES INSTRUCTIONS

1. For the apron, use HeatnBond to fuse fabric flower to apron.
2. Cut and fuse flower stems and leaves from contrasting fabrics.
3. Fuse flower appliqués over fabric flowers. Add buttons for trim. Refer to the photograph for details.
4. For gloves, cut small flowers from fabric and fuse to the cuffs. Add buttons for detail. Tie a fabric bow to center of gloves.

accessorize!

LADYBUG BAG SUPPLIES

1 MAKINGS™ craft fabric: ladybug print
⅜" Therm O Web HeatnBond iron-on adhesive
Therm O Web PeelnStick™ double-sided adhesive
Halcraft Tiny Glass Marbles
Cousins ladybug bead mix
Needle and floss, black
Assorted beads

LADYBUG BAG INSTRUCTIONS

1. Cut a 4" × 11" piece of fabric. Fold in half with right sides facing.
2. Use strips of HeatnBond to fuse together the edges of the fabric at one short edge and the long edge. Let cool and turn right side out.
3. Fold under 1 inch at the open edge of bag and glue in place.
4. Place double-sided adhesive on front and back of bag.
5. Remove paper covering and cover with the Tiny Glass Marbles. Press them into adhesive.
6. Using black floss and beads, stitch a beaded handle to bag.
7. To close the bag, make a small loop with floss at the top center back and sew bug bead on the front.

FLAG PIN SUPPLIES

1 MAKINGS™ craft fabric: flag print
Therm O Web HeatnBond iron-on adhesive
1" pin back
DMC® #5 pearl cotton, red, white and blue
3 small gold eyelets and eyelet setter
Heavy card stock or poster board
Aleene's® Thick Designer "Tacky Glue"™

FLAG PIN INSTRUCTIONS

1. Use HeatnBond to fuse the wrong side of the fabric to the card stock.
2. Cut out desired shape or design.
3. Using an eyelet setter, set three small gold eyelets near one edge of pin as shown in photo.
4. Cut a 3-inch length of each color of pearl cotton. Insert the lengths in the eyelets and knot. Trim the ends.
5. Center and glue the pin back to the wrong side of pin.

HEART PIN SUPPLIES

1 MAKINGS™ craft fabric: heart print
Therm O Web HeatnBond iron-on adhesive
Heavy card stock
3 gold eyelets and eyelet setter
Pin back
Aleene's® Thick Designer "Tacky Glue"™
Small assorted beads and charms and gold wire
Needle-nose pliers
Wire cutters

HEART PIN INSTRUCTIONS

1. Follow the instructions for flag pin, referring to the photograph for details.
2. Cut a 3-inch piece of gold wire and bend one end to make loop. Thread charm on loop and twist wire to secure charm.
3. Thread beads onto wire, then attach to an eyelet with small loop. Repeat for each eyelet.
4. Center and glue the pin back to the wrong side of pin.

denim
duo delight

OVERALLS SUPPLIES

Denim overalls
2 MAKINGS™ craft
* fabrics: cherries print*
Therm O Web HeatnBond
* iron-on adhesive*
Needle and thread

OVERALLS INSTRUCTIONS

1. Measure the distance around the bottom edge of one pant leg and add ½ inch. Use this measurement to cut two 2-inch-wide strips of fabric.
2. Use a running stitch to sew one edge of a fabric strip to the bottom of each pant leg. Fold the strip up and tack the cuff in place.
3. Apply HeatnBond to the remaining fabric. Cut out squares or rectangles to decorate the front, back and pockets of the overalls. To fray edges, remove threads one at a time until you achieve the desired amount of fraying.
4. Position shapes on the overalls and fuse.
5. To make a matching bandanna, cut an 18-inch square of fabric and fray the edges.

JEAN JACKET SUPPLIES

Denim jacket
1 MAKINGS™ craft fabric
* each: blue toile*
* and floral print*
Therm O Web HeatnBond
* iron-on adhesive*
DMC® pearl cotton, white
Needle

JEAN JACKET INSTRUCTIONS

1. Apply HeatnBond to the wrong side of fabric.
2. Make tracing-paper dragonfly patterns from the patterns on page 48. Draw around the patterns on the Heatnbond side of the fabric. Cut out the shapes.
3. Position shapes onto the back of jacket and fuse in place. Refer to the photograph for details.
4. Use pearl cotton to outline entire dragonfly with a daisy-chain stitch.
5. Sew a running stitch for the antennae, ending each with a French knot. See page 47 for a guide to these stitches.

BUGGY SHIRT SUPPLIES

Sweatshirt
1 MAKINGS™ craft fabric: bug jar print
Tulip® Slick® paint, black
Therm O Web HeatnBond iron-on adhesive
Needle and thread, black
Dress It Up® bug buttons

sweatshirt
stars

SWEATSHIRT JACKET SUPPLIES

White sweatshirt
Embroidery floss and pearl cotton, pink, lime green and teal
1 MAKINGS™ craft fabric each:
  For flower jacket— pink, turquoise and green bug
  For kitty jacket— multicolor cat print and purple
Therm O Web HeatnBond iron-on adhesive
Dress It Up® flower buttons
Tulip® Slick® paint in coordinating colors
Needles
Straight pins

BUGGY SHIRT INSTRUCTIONS

1. Prewash sweatshirt to remove sizing.
2. Cut off hem or bands from bottom of sweatshirt.
3. Cut off cuffs from sleeves.
4. Fuse HeatnBond to wrong side of fabric.
5. Cut out desired motifs from the fabric. Remove the paper backing and fuse the motifs along bottom edge of the shirt, leaving about half an inch of shirt showing.
6. Outline designs with fabric paint and let dry.
7. Cut around bottom edge of designs, cutting next to paint line.
8. Apply additional designs to shoulder area of shirt and outline with fabric paint. Let dry.
9. Fold up sleeves to form cuffs.
10. Sew buttons or other embellishments in place. Refer to photograph for details.

SWEATSHIRT JACKET INSTRUCTIONS

1. Cut off hem, band or cuff from sweatshirt. Cut sweatshirt down the center front to make opening for jacket.
2. Fold under half an inch at all cut edges and secure with straight pins.
3. Use floss to blanket-stitch all folded edges, making the stitches half an inch apart.
4. Use a second color of floss to make blanket-stitches centered between the first blanket stitches. Refer to photograph for details.
5. Fuse HeatnBond to the wrong side of each craft fabric. Make tracing patterns of the patterns on page 48. Draw around the shapes needed on the HeatnBond side of the fabric. Cut out the shapes and fuse to the jacket, referring to the photographs for placement.
6. Use pearl cotton or fabric paint to outline fabric shapes and make additional designs such as the flower curlicues and mouse tail. End curlicues with French knots.
7. Sew on buttons or other embellishments.
8. To make a floss button loop at the center top of the jacket, braid floss lengths and tack the ends of the loop to one top cover of the jacket. Sew a button directly opposite the loop on the other side, referring to the photograph for details.

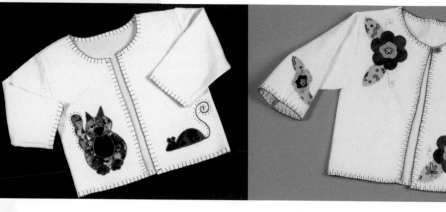

wet 'n' wild in style

T-SHIRT SUPPLIES

T-shirt
1 MAKINGS™ craft
* fabric each of four*
* coordinated designs*
Therm O Web HeatnBond
* iron-on adhesive*
Tulip® Slick® paints,
* black, red, blue and*
* white*
Shirt board or cardboard

T-SHIRT INSTRUCTIONS

1. Fuse HeatnBond to the wrong side of all craft fabrics.

2. Make tracing-paper fish patterns from the patterns on page 48. Draw around the shapes on the HeatnBond side of the fabrics, tracing as many as needed to go around the bottom of the shirt. Cut out the shapes.

3. Position fish on shirt and fuse.

4. Insert a shirt board or piece of cardboard inside the shirt to hold it flat and prevent the paint from leaking through. Decorate with dimensional paints, painting on one side at a time and letting it dry before painting the other side. Let dry flat for several hours.

5. Use black to outline the fish, draw fin and gill lines and make big dot eyes. With red dimensional paint, give each fish big lips. Make blue bubble dots rising from each mouth and add white highlights in each bubble.

6. Tear two 1½" × 10" strips of one of the fabrics. Pull up each sleeve and tie one of the strips in a knot at the top. Trim the fabric ends.

FLIP-FLOPS SUPPLIES

1 pair of brightly colored
* flip-flop sandals*
1 MAKINGS™ craft
* fabric each of four*
* coordinating designs*

FLIP-FLOPS INSTRUCTIONS

1. Tear the fabrics into 1½" x 10" strips.

2. Tie fabric strips tightly onto the flip-flops, pulling ends away from the shoe. Add strips randomly or make a pattern with the different fabrics, pushing them tightly together until the entire strap is covered.

3. Trim fabric ends evenly.

CHEER SHIRT SUPPLIES

T-shirt
***1 MAKINGS™ craft fabric
    each: cheerleader
    print and solid blue***
***Therm O Web HeatnBond
    iron-on adhesive***

CHEER SHIRT INSTRUCTIONS

1. Prewash shirt to remove sizing.
2. Cut off bottom hem from shirt.
3. Beginning at the bottom of the shirt, cut 5-inch-long slits and space half an inch apart around the shirt to fringe.
4. Tie the fringe pieces together in pairs with double knots.
5. Enlarge the patterns on the inside back cover and cut out. Trace each pattern reversed on the paper side of the HeatnBond. Cut out the shapes ¼ inch beyond the traced line. Fuse to the wrong side of the desired fabric. Cut out shapes on the traced line.
6. Position the fabric shapes on the shirt and fuse in place. Refer to the photograph for details.

cheers to the **kids!**

ONESIES SUPPLIES

Infant onesies
***Therm O Web HeatnBond
    iron-on adhesive***
⅛"-wide red ribbon
***Tulip® Slick® paints,
    red, black and silver***
Mrs. Glue™ fabric glue
***3 MAKINGS™ craft
    fabrics: coordinated
    colors***
Cardboard

ONESIES INSTRUCTIONS

1. Fuse HeatnBond to the wrong side of the craft fabrics. For dog, make a tracing paper pattern from the pattern on the inside back cover. Draw around the dog shape on the HeatnBond side of the fabric. For each ladybug, make a tracing-paper pattern from the patterns on the inside back cover. Draw around both circles on the HeatnBond side of the darkest fabric and the large circle on the HeatnBond side of the red fabric. Cut the red circle in half.
2. Referring to the photograph, position fabric shapes on the onesie and fuse in place.
3. Insert cardboard inside the onesie to keep the surface flat and prevent the paint from leaking through. Decorate shapes with dimensional paint, referring to the photograph for design details.
4. Tie tiny ribbon bows and glue to onesie at the center front of the neckline and on the collar of the dog and the ladybug necks.

kid gear

Kids and crafts are the perfect combination for creative fun and quality time with family and friends. Add bright and whimsical fabrics, and you can't go wrong! Pick a project, and you'll find craft fabrics are just the right size for little hands and big imaginations.

SOCCER PILLOW SUPPLIES

Makes one pillow

1 MAKINGS™ craft fabric: blue or red
1 MAKINGS™ craft fabric: soccer print
⅜" Therm O Web HeatnBond iron-on adhesive tape
1 pkg of Poly-Fil extra-loft batting

SOCCER PILLOW INSTRUCTIONS

1. Place soccer print face up on ironing board. Iron on the adhesive to 3 edges, two long sides and one short side, following instructions on the package.
2. Place red or blue fabric right side down on the soccer fabric. Iron edges with adhesive to bond fabric.
3. Turn remaining edge to the outside. Press. Turn pillow so right sides are on outside. Apply iron-on adhesive to open edge.
4. Fold batting into thirds, so it measures about 15" × 20". Cut into 3 pieces. Stuff into pillow cover.
5. Remove adhesive paper from remaining edge. Place edges together and press to secure and close the pillow.

boys will be boys

TREASURE BOX SUPPLIES

Plaid® Mod Podge®, matte
2 MAKINGS™ craft fabrics: transportation print
Pencil box
Delta Ceramcoat® acrylic paint, black
5 Lara's unfinished wooden knobs
Hot-glue gun and glue sticks

TREASURE BOX INSTRUCTIONS

1. Cut three 2¼" × 22" strips of fabric.
2. Cut the strips to fit the box sides, on the inside and outside surfaces.
3. For the inside bottom and lid, cut three 5½" × 8¾" rectangles from the remaining fabric, keeping in mind the direction of the design on the fabric.
4. Apply Mod Podge to the top of the lid and the edges inside of lid. Center and smooth a fabric rectangle on outside of lid allowing fabric to go around all edges of box. Repeat to cover all inside and outside surfaces of the box. Trim outside edge pieces to fit the ends of the box, allowing the top edge to go into the inside of the box. Decoupage into place with Mod Podge.
5. Apply a coat of Mod Podge to all fabric surfaces to seal. Prop the box balanced on an edge with the lid open to dry. If any edges of the box show, paint with a matching color.
6. Paint knobs and let dry. Glue knobs onto finished box with hot glue for feet and lid knob.

PHOTO ALBUM SUPPLIES

Small photograph album

1 MAKINGS™ craft fabric: sports print

Batting

1 yard of grosgrain ribbon

Iron-on soccer ball appliqué

Hot-glue gun and glue sticks

Soccer-ball beads

Mrs. Glue™ fabric glue

PHOTO ALBUM INSTRUCTIONS

1. Cut batting to fit the front, back and spine of the photo album.
2. Center opened photo album on the wrong side of the fabric. Trace around the album. Cut out 2 inches beyond the drawn lines.
3. Center batting and fabric on the album. Tightly pull the fabric edges to the inside of the album and glue in place with hot glue.
4. Cut two pieces of fabric to fit on the inside front and back covers. Glue in place.
5. Cut the ribbon in half. Glue one end of each ribbon length to the album center front and back, turning under the raw end. Fuse the appliqué over the ribbon end on the front.
6. Add beads to the ribbon ends. Refer to the photograph for details.

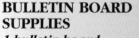

BULLETIN BOARD SUPPLIES

1 bulletin board (22½" × 16½")

1 MAKINGS™ craft fabric each: baseball and stars print

Tulip® Slick® paint, white

Delta Ceramcoat® acrylic paint, red opaque

Xyron™ machine with laminate

Stapler

BULLETIN BOARD INSTRUCTIONS

1. Paint frame of bulletin board. Let dry.
2. Cut an 8¼" × 22" strip of one fabric and laminate it with the Xyron machine. Trim the laminated strip to fit half of the bulletin board.
3. Cut an 8¼" × 22" strip of the second fabric. Press under edges to fit half of the bulletin board, allowing the fabric to overlap slightly in the center.
4. Attach fabric strip and laminated strip to the bulletin board by stapling the edges next to the frame.
5. Run a bead of white paint around the inside edges of the frame.
6. Use only a dry-erase pen on the laminated surface.

CAP RACK SUPPLIES

1 peg rack, unpainted wood
1 Makings™ craft fabric: blue/white star print
Delta Ceramcoat® acrylic paint, red and white
Plaid® Mod Podge®, matte

INITIALS SUPPLIES

2 six-inch wooden letters
1 MAKINGS™ craft fabric each: blue and red
Plaid® Mod Podge®, matte
Plaid® Mod Podge®, gloss

CAP RACK INSTRUCTIONS

1. Paint the outside edge of the rack and all pegs. Refer to the photograph for details. Let dry.
2. Cut fabric into triangles and squares. Apply fabric pieces to the flat front of the rack with Mod Podge one at a time, overlapping the edges to completely cover the rack surface.
3. Apply additional Mod Podge to finished fabric surface to secure.

INITIALS INSTRUCTIONS

1. Cut each piece of fabric into small, triangular shapes.
2. Coat the back of each fabric shape with matte Mod Podge and apply it to the letter surface.
3. Continue gluing the shapes onto the letter until the entire letter is covered. Trim excess fabric.
4. Coat the entire covered letter with gloss Mod Podge. Let dry.

DOOR HANGER SUPPLIES

1 door hanger
1 MAKINGS™ craft fabric: star print
Making Memories Creative Letters vinyl letters
Tulip® Slick® paint, yellow
Plaid® Mod Podge®, matte

DOOR HANGER SUPPLIES

1. Cut two pieces of fabric slightly larger than the door hanger. Lay both pieces right sides together.
2. Place door hanger over the fabric. Using a rotary cutter, cut, following the shape of the hanger.
3. Apply Mod Podge to both sides of the hanger.
4. Place a fabric piece on the hanger, stretching to fit. Do the same for the back side. Let dry.
5. Position letters to spell "my room" or words of your choice on the hanger.
6. Use dimensional paint to outline or accent the letters. Let dry.
7. Paint entire hanger with Mod Podge. Let dry. Outline edges of hanger with dimensional paint.

Kid Gear

PILLOW SUPPLIES
10-inch pillow form
1 MAKINGS™ craft fabric
each: solid and print

PILLOW INSTRUCTIONS
1. Cut an 18" × 18" square from each fabric.
2. With right sides together, place the fabric squares on a flat surface. Center the pillow form on the squares. Use a pencil to draw around the pillow form.
3. Remove the pillow form. Beginning at the edge of the fabric, cut slits half an inch apart up to the pencil line. Continue along edges of the layered squares.
4. Place a fabric square on each side of the pillow form with right sides out.
5. Tie strips together tightly to cover the form.

groovy little gifts

BOOKMARK SUPPLIES
Pearl cotton
Small gold eyelets and eyelet setter
1 MAKINGS™ craft fabric
Heavy card stock
Assorted glass beads
Therm O Web HeatnBond iron-on adhesive

BOOKMARK INSTRUCTIONS
1. Use HeatnBond to fuse the wrong side of the fabric to the card stock. Cut out desired shape or design.
2. Decorate bookmarks with eyelets, beads and pearl cotton. Thread pearl cotton through eyelets. Tie beads at ends of pearl cotton. Refer to the photographs for ideas.

BOOK COVER SUPPLIES

1 MAKINGS™ craft fabric:
  Harlequin print
⅝"-wide grosgrain ribbon,
  red
Mrs. Glue™ fabric glue
Large bead (to fit double
  ribbon width)
Therm O Web HeatnBond
  iron-on adhesive

BOOK COVER INSTRUCTIONS

1. Open book and lay on the wrong side of the fabric with 1 inch of fabric at the top and 5 inches at the sides.
2. Trace around the book. Cut out fabric half an inch beyond the top and bottom lines and 5 inches beyond the left and right lines.
3. Press under ¼ inch on all edges and secure with HeatnBond.
4. Fuse a strip of HeatnBond tape vertically along the fabric center spine.
5. Measure and cut the ribbon twice the length of the spine plus 6 inches. Lay the ribbon centered along HeatnBond strip on spine. Press to secure.
6. Fold in about 4 to 5 inches at the left and right edge of the fabric, creating inside pockets. Apply a line of glue along the top and bottom edge of each pocket to secure. Let dry.
7. Measure the width of the fabric cover and cut a length of ribbon three times this measurement. Glue the ribbon centered on the fabric cover. Let dry flat.
8. Thread both ends of the the ribbon through the bead and tie the ribbon together 2 inches from the ends.
9. Trim all ribbon ends at an angle.

TEACHER'S GIFT SUPPLIES

1 MAKINGS™ craft
  fabric: ABC print
¾ yard grosgrain
  ribbon
Dress It Up® school
  buttons
Therm O Web
  HeatnBond iron-on
  adhesive
DMC® floss, red
Mrs. Glue™ fabric glue

TEACHER'S GIFT INSTRUCTIONS

1. Press under half an inch on each edge of the 18" × 22" fabric and secure with ⅜-inch-wide HeatnBond.
2. With the 22-inch length horizontal, lay the fabric right side down. Fold the top edge down 9 inches from the top.
3. Fold up the bottom 4 inches to create a pocket.
4. Using the floss, sew running stitches to divide the large pocket into small pockets to accommodate note cards, a ruler, pencils and other school supplies. Fold the fabric case into overlapping thirds.
5. With the case folded, position ribbon around the case, making equal tails on the open edge. Glue the ribbon in place.
6. Sew buttons in place. Tie. Refer to the photograph for details.

let's play!

Young fabric crafters don't need to handle a needle and thread to create these easy and fun projects.

PET SCARF SUPPLIES

1 MAKINGS™ craft fabric: dog print
⅜"-wide Therm O Web HeatnBond iron-on adhesive
Rickrack ribbon
Mrs. Glue™ fabric glue
Iron-on letters, ¼" tall

PET SCARF INSTRUCTIONS

1. Cut an 18-inch square of fabric.
2. Fold the square in half diagonally with the right sides together. Use strips of HeatnBond to fuse together the raw edges, leaving a 3-inch opening on one edge for turning.
3. Turn scarf right side out and close opening with HeatnBond.
4. Glue rickrack along the edges of the scarf.
5. Spell pet's name or message of your choice with letters. Iron in place following manufacturer's instructions.

LEASH SUPPLIES

Dog leash
1 MAKINGS™ craft fabric: green dot print
⅜"-wide Therm O Web HeatnBond iron-on adhesive
Hot-glue gun and glue sticks

LEASH INSTRUCTIONS

1. Cut four 2" × 22" strips of fabric.
2. Use HeatnBond to fuse the short edges of strips together, creating one long strip. Press seams to one side.
3. Press under half an inch along one long edge of the strip.
4. Apply a strip of HeatnBond to the fold of the fabric strip.
5. Overlap half an inch on the remaining long edge with the folded edge. Fuse in place, creating a fabric tube.
6. Turn under half an inch at the open ends of the tube.
7. Slide tube over leash, scrunching the fabric as you do.
8. Glue the top and bottom with hot glue to secure.

here kitty, kitty...

PLACE MAT SUPPLIES
*1 MAKINGS™ craft fabric
  each: kitty print
  and muslin*
Plaid® Mod Podge®, matte
Foam paintbrush

PET BOWL SUPPLIES
*Pet-bowl personalizing
  kit*

PLACE MAT INSTRUCTIONS
1. Create a 16" × 20" oval pattern with cardboard or tracing paper.
  Use the pattern to cut one oval from the printed fabric
  and one from the muslin.
2. Apply Mod Podge to the wrong side of each oval and stick
  them together. Let dry.
3. Apply Mod Podge to one side of the mat and let dry. Decoupage the
  remaining side and let dry.
4. Trim edges if necessary.

PET BOWL INSTRUCTIONS
1. Following directions on pet-dish kit, draw a design to
  match the place-mat fabric as shown.
2. Bake according to manufacturer's directions.

funky and fun!

WASTEBASKET SUPPLIES

1 MAKINGS™ craft fabric
each of three
coordinating colors
Assorted DecoColor
painter's pens, orange,
ultramarine blue
and lime
Purchased wastebasket
with cutouts, white
Awl or metal punch,
optional

LAMP SUPPLIES

1 MAKINGS™ craft fabric
each of three
coordinating colors
⅝" hole punch
Small lamp and shade
Plaid® Mod Podge®, matte
Paint supplies (above)

WASTEBASKET INSTRUCTIONS

1. If wastebasket does not have holes along the upper rim, use an awl or punch to make evenly spaced holes about half an inch apart.
2. Tear fabrics into 1-inch strips.
3. Insert three strips into each hole. Tie each strip into a knot, and trim ends to 3 inches beyond the knot.
4. Repeat until all holes are filled.
5. Decorate with painter's pens, referring to photograph for ideas.

LAMP INSTRUCTIONS

1. Punch holes about one inch apart along the bottom edge of the lampshade.
2. Tear fabrics into 1 inch strips.
3. Insert three strips into each hole and tie each into a knot.
4. Trim the ends 2 inches beyond the knot.
5. Draw design on shade with paint pens, referring to photograph for ideas.
6. Cut a piece of fabric to cover the stem of the lamp. Apply Mod Podge to secure fabric in place.

FLOOR CLOTH SUPPLIES

Fredrix® preprimed 2' × 3' canvas floor cloth
2 MAKINGS™ craft fabrics each: blue wave stripe, orange/yellow-check
1 MAKINGS™ craft fabric: multicolor stripe
2 DecoColor wide-tip painter's pens, yellow and blue
Plaid® Mod Podge®, matte
Minwax Polycrylic finish, satin

FLOOR CLOTH INSTRUCTIONS

1. Make a tracing-paper pattern of the triangle pattern on the inside back cover.
2. Use the pattern to cut 19 triangles from the blue wave fabric, 12 triangles from the orange/yellow fabric and 9 triangles from the striped fabric.
3. Turn over the pattern and cut the same number of triangles reversed from each of the fabrics.
4. Starting at the center of the floor cloth, lay out the fabric triangles, referring to the photograph for placement.
5. Decoupage pieces onto floor cloth, working in small sections.
6. Trim floor cloth to make edges even if necessary.
7. Apply Mod Podge to the entire floor cloth. Let dry.
8. Draw yellow lines between triangles with painter's pen. Paint outside edges of cloth blue. Let dry.
9. Apply at least three coats of polycrylic finish to the front of the cloth, allowing manufacturer's dry time between each coat.

the teen scene

STOOL SUPPLIES

Wood stool
1 MAKINGS™ craft fabric: multicolor stripe
Plaid® Mod Podge®, matte
Minwax Polycrylic finish, satin
Delta Ceramcoat® acrylic paint, yellow, teal and purple
DecoColor painter's pens, orange, ultramarine blue, lime green
Heavy-duty staple gun

STOOL INSTRUCTIONS

1. Paint the stool legs with acrylic paints, referring to the photograph for ideas. When paint is dry, decorate with paint pens. Let dry.
2. Place fabric right side down on a flat surface. Turn the stool upside down on the fabric. Trace around the seat with a pencil. Cut out the fabric circle 3 inches beyond the drawn line.
3. Use Mod Podge to adhere fabric on top and sides of stool seat.
4. Secure fabric underneath seat with staples.

Kid Gear

baubles, bottles and beads

FRAME SUPPLIES

1 4" × 6" plastic picture frame
1 MAKINGS™ craft fabric: princess/heart print
4" × 6" poster board
Mrs. Glue™ fabric glue
Double-sided adhesive
Assorted rhinestones

NECKLACE SUPPLIES

1 MAKINGS™ craft fabric: pink/blue splatter
Therm O Web HeatnBond iron-on adhesive
Metal knitting needle
¾" × 1" large-hole faceted acrylic beads
Satin beading cord

FRAME INSTRUCTIONS

1. Cut poster board to 4" × 6" using the pattern provided with the frame.
2. Measure and cut fabric to 4" × 6" to fit over the poster board. Attach the fabric to the board with fabric glue. Trim.
3. Place photo in center of fabric-covered board with glue or double-sided tape. Slide finished board into the photo frame.
4. Cut individual hearts out of fabric and glue the front of the frame. Refer to the photo for details.
5. Glue rhinestones to the hearts and frame.

NECKLACE INSTRUCTIONS

1. Trace ¾" × 1" rectangles onto HeatnBond. Fuse to wrong side of fabric.
2. Cut out rectangles, tapering at one end.
3. Remove paper backing from tapered end leaving 1" of paper at opposite end.
4. Roll fabric onto knitting needle with paper on the needle, ending with tapering to the
5. With warm iron, heat set bead. Slip bead o
6. Make desired number of beads. String fabri onto cord alternating with faceted acrylic

DECORATIVE BOTTLES SUPPLIES

Craft Bottles
Assorted MAKINGS™ craft
fabrics
Wild Wire copper wire in
assorted colors
Bead Heaven glass and
wire beads
Therm O Web HeatnBond
iron-on adhesive

DECORATIVE BOTTLES INSTRUCTIONS

1. Twist wire around bottle. Add beads.
2. Tie a fabric bow at the top or fuse a strip of fabric around the bottle using HeatnBond.

sweet boutique

With the many styles of beads, trims and craft fabrics today, kids can be proud of the one-of-a-kind gifts and treasures they can create.

BEANBAG GAME INSTRUCTIONS

1. Trace and cut out all frog and turtle patterns provided on the inside back cover.

2. For the frog, cut two frog bodies from green/yellow stripe fabric, four frog legs from light green felt, and one tongue from red felt. For the turtle, cut two turtle bodies from green swirls fabric and four turtle legs, one head and one tail from dark green felt.

3. To assemble beanbags, place one turtle body right side up on work surface. Position legs, head and tail on body with the felt pieces toward the center of the body and the outer edges even. Glue in place. Apply a line of glue along the outer edge of body, leaving a 2-inch opening for turning. Place the remaining turtle body right side down on the first, covering the felt pieces. Press the glued area together and let dry. Repeat for the frog body.

4. When dry, turn assembled felt bodies right side out. Place beanbag inserts inside. Fold in open edges and glue. Let dry.

5. Glue tiny white pom-poms on turtle legs and tiny red pom-poms on frog legs. Glue tiny black pom-poms for the noses.

6. Glue the eyes on black felt and cut around leaving a small black border. Glue the smaller eyes on the turtle and larger eyes on the frog. Glue on the frog's red tongue and let dry.

7. For the pond and pad, cut the blue felt in a large wavy shape, referring to the photograph.

8. Apply HeatnBond to the wrong side of all remaining fabrics.

9. Cut out the ladybug fabric in several pieces in random wavy shapes. Overlap the pieces on the center of blue felt to make main lily pad. Fuse in place.

10. For the smaller lily pad, cut the green swirls fabric in several smaller wavy shapes. Position the pieces on the ladybug fabric and fuse in place.

11. Cut flower petals out of yellow and yellow/orange fabrics (about 7 of each). Arrange the petals on the green swirls fabric in a flower shape, overlapping and alternating fabrics. Fuse in place.

12. Cut out a red center. Fuse to center of the flower.

13. Punch holes 1½ inches apart around the edge of the blue felt.

14. Thread cording through the holes and tie at the end of the cords with an overhand knot.

15. Place the beanbags in the center of the lily pad and pull up the cording to store the game.

BEANBAG GAME SUPPLIES

1 sq. yd. of blue felt
1 MAKINGS™ craft fabric each: ladybug print, green swirls print, yellow print, yellow/orange swirl print, red print, green/yellow stripe print
Small felt pieces, light green, dark green, black and red
Tiny pom-poms, black, red and white
2 tiny wiggle eyes
2 ⅜"-diameter wiggle eyes
3 yds. satin cording, green
⅛" hole punch
Therm O Web HeatnBond iron-on adhesive
Premade beanbag inserts
Mrs. Glue™ fabric glue

celebrate!
special days

With colorful and festive craft fabrics and these so-simple projects, you can celebrate special occasions with unique gifts and memorable decorations. Let the crafting and the partying begin!

CENTERPIECE SUPPLIES

1 MAKINGS™ craft fabrics
  each: yellow vintage,
  yellow, green swirls
1 stiffened felt square
  each, yellow and green
³⁄₁₆" × 12" dowel rods
Therm O Web HeatnBond
  iron-on adhesive
Large buttons
Aleene's® Thick Designer
  "Tacky Glue"™
Tulip® Slick® paints, red
  and green
4" × 8" × 2" Styrofoam
  block
4 picket fence sections
Delta Ceramcoat®
  acrylic paint, white
Sheet of Spanish moss
Floral pins

CENTERPIECE INSTRUCTIONS

1. Apply HeatnBond to fabrics. Iron fabric onto felt. Make flower patterns and cut desired flowers and leaves from fabrics.
2. Make a fabric yo-yo for each flower center and glue to flowers. See page 41 for yo-yo instructions. Glue a button to each center.
3. Make two small 2-inch slits in centers of flowers and center of stem and insert dowel rods.
4. Use red fabric paint to outline edges of flowers and green to outline leaves. Let dry.
5. Separate picket-fence sections into four sections. Paint white and let dry.
6. Cover Styrofoam with Spanish moss.
7. Glue picket-fence sections around moss-covered Styrofoam. Secure with floral pins
8. Insert flowers into Styrofoam.

flower power

PLACE MATS SUPPLIES

Assorted MAKINGS™ craft
  fabrics: coordinated
  with flower
  centerpiece
Therm O Web HeatnBond
  iron-on adhesive
scissors, straight and
  wave-edged
Tulip® Slick® paints,
  assorted colors

FLOWER PLACE MATS INSTRUCTIONS

1. Fuse one piece of each coordinating set of fabrics to the HeatnBond.
2. Cut out flowers, centers and leaves using your patterns for the centerpiece .
3. With wavy-edged scissors, cut rectangles as large as possible with remaining fused fabric for place mats. Fuse together, coordinating fronts and backs.
4. Place one coordinating flower, with two leaves and a center on each place mat and press.
5. Outline flowers and leaves with fabric paint.

BASKET SUPPLIES
Basket
Hirschberg fringe
Hot-glue gun and glue sticks

SALT JAR SUPPLIES
Small canning jar
Batting
Pinking sheers
1 MAKINGS™ craft fabric
each: muslin and
grape print
Therm O Web HeatnBond
iron-on adhesive
Mrs. Glue™ fabric glue

WINE BOTTLE BAG SUPPLIES
1 MAKINGS™ craft
fabric: grape print
Therm O Web HeatnBond
iron-on adhesive
Mini Grapevine Wreath

BASKET INSTRUCTIONS
1. Glue fringe onto basket with hot glue.

SALT JAR INSTRUCTIONS
1. Cut a 6-inch circle of muslin with pinking sheers.
2. Cut a 6-inch circle of batting and glue onto jar lid.
3. Center circle of muslin over jar lid and screw the jar ring into place.
4. Tear a 12" × 1" strip of desired fabric. Apply HeatnBond and fold over raw edges. Press to the width of the jar ring. Tie into place.

WINE BOTTLE BAG INSTRUCTIONS
1. Cut fabric to 16" × 13".
2. Fold right sides of fabric in half. Apply HeatnBond tape to the seam side and bottom of fabric.
3. Turn under top hem 1 inch and fuse with HeatnBond.
4. Turn fabric right side out.

welcome gift

PLACE CARD SUPPLIES
2" terra-cotta pot
1 MAKINGS™ craft fabric
each: yellow, green swirls
3" × 8" Therm O Web
HeatnBond iron-on
adhesive
Floral foam
Sheet of Spanish moss
6" piece of ⅛" dowel
Delta Ceramcoat® acrylic
paint, green
Tulip® Slick® paints, green
and red
1" button
Hot-glue gun and
glue sticks

PLACE CARD INSTRUCTIONS
1. Paint dowel green and let dry.
2. Fill pot with floral foam.
3. Write name on pot rim with green dimensional paint. Let dry.
4. Trace and cut out patterns for small flower and small leaves.
5. Fuse flower fabrics together and fuse leaf fabrics together with HeatnBond.
6. Trace and cut out flower and leaves.
7. Cut two small slits horizontally about 1 inch apart at center of flower and at center of leaves
8. Weave dowel through the leaf and then through the flower, with end of dowel at the back of the flower. Glue flower and leaf in place.
9. Outline flower and make veins with red dimensional paint.
10. Glue button to center of flower and glue dowel into pot.
11. Glue moss on top of floral foam around dowel.

baby
special delivery

SIPPEE CUP SUPPLIES
*Plastic sippee cup with
   paper decorative
   insert*
*1 MAKINGS™ craft fabric:
   baby plaid*
*Therm O Web HeatnBond
   iron-on adhesive*

SIPPEE CUP INSTRUCTIONS
1. Take out paper label and use as a pattern to cut fabric adding
   2 inches to the length.
2. Fuse HeatnBond to fabric.
3. Trim edges neatly, leaving on paper backing, and place in cup.

BIB SUPPLIES
*2 bibs with cross-
   stitching strip*
*1 MAKINGS™ craft fabric:
   baby print*
*Therm O Web HeatnBond
   iron-on adhesive*

BIB INSTRUCTIONS
1. Cut strip of fabric with desired designs to fit in
   cross-stitch section on the bib.
2. Apply HeatnBond to fabric strip, trimming the edges neatly.
3. Press fabric onto bib cross-stitch section, tucking edges
   under the seamed edge.

BABY BOX SUPPLIES

Large round papier-maché box

1 MAKINGS™ craft fabric each: baby plaid and baby stripe

2 yds of 1½"-wide ribbon

2 ⅜" fabric grommets and grommet setter

2 ½"-diameter beads

1 pkg. wide rickrack, pastel multicolored

Therm O Web HeatnBond iron-on adhesive

Delta Ceramcoat® acrylic paint, baby blue

Aleene's® Thick Designer "Tacky Glue"™

BABY BOX INSTRUCTIONS

1. Paint inside of box, lid rim and inside of lid. Let dry.
2. Measure height and distance around the box. Cut plaid fabric to fit.
3. Cut a piece of HeatnBond to fit and fuse it to the fabric.
4. Fuse fabric onto outside of box to secure.
5. Lay the lid flat on wrong side of striped fabric. Cut a square slightly larger than the top of the lid.
6. Fuse HeatnBond to the lid fabric.
7. Lay lid on the fabric again and trace around lid. Cut out circle of fabric and fuse to the outside of the lid top.
8. Apply a grommet to opposite sides of the box, about three-fourths of the way up.
9. Cut ribbon in half. Working from the outside, thread a ribbon length through a grommet. Thread a bead on the ribbon ends inside the box and tie a knot. Repeat with the opposite side.
10. For each side, tie a knot in the ribbon outside the box next to the grommet. Trim ribbon ends at an angle.
11. Center and glue the rickrack trim around the rim of the lid.
12. Put the lid on the box and pull ribbons up to tie into a big bow.

BABY BAG SUPPLIES

Large natural-colored canvas bag

1 MAKINGS™ craft fabric each of two coordinating colors

Needle and white thread

2" Lara's wooden disk, unpainted

1½ yds. of 1½"-wide ribbon, pink plaid

11 ⅜" fabric grommets

Grommet setter

Delta Ceramcoat® acrylic paint, pink

ProvoCraft wood "baby" trim

Tulip® Slick® paints, lime and olive

½"-wide flat paint brush

Liner brush

Mrs. Glue™ fabric glue

BABY BAG INSTRUCTIONS

1. Apply 11 grommets, evenly spaced around top rim of bag as shown. Apply two grommets in the center front about 2 inches apart for the bow. Space grommets at each side so that the ribbon will go around the outside past the side seams.
2. Weave ribbon through grommets and tie a bow at center front. Cut a V in each ribbon end.
3. Cut an 18-inch–diameter circle of fabric to make a large yo-yo and a 10-inch-diameter circle to make a smaller yo-yo. Refer to yo-yo instructions below.
4. Glue yo-yos onto front of bag, referring to the photograph.
5. Paint leaves on bag front with fabric paints.
6. Paint wooden disk with acrylic paint. Let dry.
7. Glue disk to the center of the smaller yo-yo.
8. Glue small wooden "baby" piece in center of disk.

YO-YOS!

To make fabric yo-yos, cut a circle from fabric. Using a needle and thread, make a running stitch ¼ inch from the edge. Gently pull the thread while holding the center of the fabric. The edges will come to the center. Knot thread to create a finished edge on your yo-yo circle.

pinwheel party

PINWHEEL NAPKIN RINGS SUPPLIES

*1 MAKINGS™ craft fabric
each: orange and
yellow check, yellow,
yellow with orange
swirl, orange,
blue/turquoise stripe,
turquoise/blue slash,
lime green/yellow
stripe, lime green*
*Therm O Web HeatnBond
iron-on adhesive*
⅛" hole punch
¼" brads, colored
*Scissors, straight or
wavy edged*
*Tulip® Slick® paint, red
and green*
Stapler
Lightweight cardboard

PINWHEEL NAPKIN RINGS INSTRUCTIONS

1. Cut four strips of fabric (3" × 7") to coordinate
   with pinwheels as shown.
2. Fold in sides of strips and press to fuse. Trim ends.
   Overlap ends to make rings and staple to hold.
3. Using the small pinwheel pattern provided on the inside
   back cover, trace and cut out five cardboard pieces.
4. Fuse fabric to each side of the cardboard shapes with HeatnBond,
   putting coordinating fabrics on opposite sides.
5. Cut slices in pinwheel squares as shown on pattern.
6. Punch a hole in the center of each pinwheel and then in
   every other point.
7. Punch a ⅛-inch hole in each ring, centered next to the staple.
8. Thread a brad through each hole in the points in a pinwheel,
   through the center hole, and then through the hole in the ring.
   Flatten the back of brad to fasten.

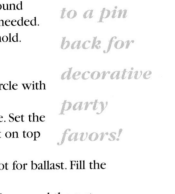

CENTERPIECE SUPPLIES

6"-diameter terra-cotta pot
1 MAKINGS™ craft fabric each: orange/yellow check, yellow, yellow with orange swirl, orange, blue/turquoise stripe, turquoise/blue slash, lime green/yellow stripe, lime green
Therm O Web HeatnBond iron-on adhesive
⅛" hole punch
Assorted colors of ¼" brads
1 pkg. of 12" × ¼" dowels
24" length of 20-gauge wire
Elastic thread and large-eye needle
Lightweight cardboard
Hot-glue gun and glue sticks
Batting
Floral foam
Glass marbles

CENTERPIECE INSTRUCTIONS

1. Using the larger pinwheel pattern provided on the inside back cover, trace and cut out five cardboard pieces.
2. Fuse fabric to each side of the cardboard shapes with HeatnBond, putting coordinating fabrics on opposite sides.
3. Cut slices in each pinwheel as shown on pattern.
4. Punch a ⅛-inch hole in the center of each pinwheel and then in every other point.
5. Thread a brad through each hole in the points in a pinwheel, then through the center hole. Flatten back of brad to fasten.
6. Cut five 8-inch lengths of wire.
7. Fold a length of wire in half and wrap the center around the back of the brad and then tightly around dowel, about 1 inch from one end. Trim ends if needed. Place a drop of hot glue on each wire wrap to hold.
8. Cut a 12½-inch-diameter circle of batting and coordinating fabric.
9. Baste half an inch from the edge of the fabric circle with the elastic thread.
10. Lay the fabric, right side down, on a flat surface. Set the batting on the fabric and center the flower pot on top of the batting.
11. Put a few glass marbles in the bottom of the pot for ballast. Fill the pot to the top with floral foam.
12. Pull the threads to tighten the batting and fabric around the pot. Work with it until it is smooth and round. Knot the elastic thread and trim off excess.
13. Stick pinwheels in foam and add a scrap piece of fabric on top of the foam to cover, as shown.
14. Fuse two 2" × 22" strips of coordinating fabrics together with HeatnBond and trim edges.
15. Knot fabric strip around the top of the fabric and batting—or flip over one end, as shown and pull tight. Trim ends and glue in place.

Make tiny pinwheels and apply to a pin back for decorative party favors!

CARD AND GIFT BAG SUPPLIES

Card and envelope
Scissors
Pinking sheers
Yellow card stock
Decorative-edge scissors
DMC® pearl cotton, blue
Therm O Web HeatnBond iron-on adhesive
2 MAKINGS™ craft fabric: balloon print
Mrs. Glue™ fabric glue

CARD INSTRUCTIONS

1. Apply HeatnBond to fabric.
2. Cut out desired design from fabric and iron onto card stock. Refer to photograph for details.
3. Cut pearl cotton, tie into bows and glue onto card as shown.
4. Glue card stock onto premade card.

GIFT BAG INSTRUCTIONS

1. Cut fabric to gift size with pinking sheers.
2. Place gift inside, pull up sides to top and tie with pearl cotton.

JEWELRY BOX SUPPLIES

Walnut Hollow® large oval box

1 MAKINGS™ craft fabric: rose floral print

DecoArt® Americana acrylic paint

Delta Ceramcoat® crackle paint medium

Delta Ceramcoat® Gleams paint, silver

Batting

Therm O Web HeatnBond iron-on adhesive

Mat board

Aleene's® Original "Tacky Glue"™

Spray acrylic varnish

Sandpaper

Liquitex® acrylic gesso paint, white

½" wide rhinestone trim

JEWELRY BOX INSTRUCTIONS

1. Sand and paint box with gesso paint. Let dry.
2. Paint box with silver paint. Let dry.
3. Paint box with crackle medium and rose-pink paint. Let dry.
4. Apply a coat of spray varnish.
5. With fabric glue, adhere an oval of batting to the top of the lid.
6. Cover batting with an oval of fabric, using a gathering thread to secure and gluing the edges to the underside of the lid.
7. Glue rhinestone trim around outside edge.
8. Line inside of box with a fabric-covered oval mat board and a strip of fabric to cover the interior sides.

SACHETS SUPPLIES

1 MAKINGS™ craft fabric each: pink check and blue floral

Potpourri

Floral wire

Assorted ribbon

Small painted wood trims

9½" × 4" envelope

Therm O Web HeatnBond iron-on adhesive

Assorted small artificial flowers

Pinking shears

SACHETS INSTRUCTIONS

1. For the pink sachet, cut a circle of fabric with pinking shears.
2. Add potpourri to center.
3. Hand-gather the fabric around the potpourri and secure it with floral wire or thread.
4. Add ribbon bow and small purchased painted wood trim.
5. For the blue sachet, add potpourri to a 9½" × 4" business-size envelope. Seal.
6. Fold the envelope in half.
7. Apply HeatnBond to the fabric. Cut a piece of fabric to wrap the folded envelope package.
8. Add a ribbon bow and artificial flowers for trim.

Crafting with fabric

CREATING A WORK AREA

Before beginning your project, find a large, flat surface to use as your work area. Try to select an area with adequate lighting where you can work uninterrupted without having to clean up mid-project. If you use spray adhesive, be sure to work in a well-ventilated area. Read through the instructions thoroughly and gather all the supplies you need. Keep your work surface uncluttered by putting away any items not in use. If the project calls for paint or glue, protect the work surface with newspaper, waxed paper or large paper grocery bags laid flat (cut along one of the corner creases and the bottom so it lies flat).

SELECTING TOOLS TO USE

When working with fabrics, scissors are the most important purchase you make. Save yourself frustration and disappointment by investing in a good quality, sharp fabric scissors. Tie a ribbon around one of the handles as a reminder to use this scissors only for cutting fabric; you will dull the blades if you use them for any other purpose. In addition, a strong crafts scissors is essential for cutting paper, cardboard and plastic. Another option is a pinking shears that creates a decorative zigzag pattern on fabric edges and also prevents fraying. If you cut many straight-edged shapes, a rotary cutter, self-healing cutting mat, and clear

acrylic ruler are good investments. These tools provide the crafter with speed and accuracy. Another cutting tool to consider is a crafts knife with a sharp blade, which works well for reaching into corners.

For marking tools, use a sharp No. 2 pencil to lightly trace around patterns on light-colored fabric and a white dressmaker's pencil on dark-colored fabric. Scout your local crafts store to find other marking tools for your project, such as erasable fabric markers.

Other general supplies needed are straight pins for securing fabrics, an iron and ironing board, liquid seam sealant to seal the fabric edges and prevent fraying, needles, and template material, such as plastic or cardboard.

COORDINATING FABRICS

When selecting fabrics, the most important rule is to not be afraid of experimenting. Play with combinations of colors, patterns and textures. Be guided by your desired finished look. Choose cotton fabrics because they press and crease well. Take into account the size of the pattern on printed fabric and try to select a pattern that will not overwhelm the size of the project. Small fabric patterns are versatile and work well on almost all projects. Large patterns are limiting, and you will not see the shape on small pieces.

PREPARING FABRICS

It is important to wash, dry and press fabric before using it if the finished project is one that will be washed or if you will be painting on the fabric. Wash the fabric in warm water with a mild detergent and dry in a clothes dryer at medium setting. This shrinks the fabric and removes any excess dye. Washing also removes any finishes or sizing that prevents paints from sticking.

TRACING

The patterns included in this book are half size. Enlarge them to 200 percent with a photocopy machine, or you may enlarge each by hand on graph paper. It may be necessary to retrace each enlarged pattern piece individually onto tracing paper to make separate pattern pieces. Cut out the individual tracing-paper pattern pieces. Pin the tracing-paper pattern pieces onto fabric, or trace the shapes onto cardboard or plastic and cut out for firmer patterns. Firmer patterns are suggested if you will be tracing around it or using the pattern piece many times.

CUTTING

Lay out the pressed fabric on a flat surface. Use straight pins to pin the tracing-paper pattern pieces onto the fabrics or to position heavier patterns securely. Use a fabric scissors to cut out the fabric shapes along the outside edges of the pattern pieces. Cut as many of each shape as indicated on the pattern or in the instructions.

If you are cutting many straight-edged shapes from several fabrics, such as squares and rectangles, a rotary cutter will save you time. Use caution when cutting with a rotary cutter, as the blade is extremely sharp. Always cut away from yourself and use the blade guard whenever the cutter is not in use, even for just a moment. Keep it well out of children's reach.

To use the rotary cutter, place the pressed fabric on a self-healing cutting mat. You may layer fabrics to cut the same shape from several fabrics at the same time. Align the fabric with a horizontal line on the cutting mat. Place the clear acrylic ruler over the fabric, aligning the ruler with a vertical line on the mat. Hold the cutter in your dominant hand. Firmly press on the ruler with the fingertips of your other hand. To keep the ruler from sliding, let your pinky finger rest firmly on the fabric. Cut along the edge of the ruler. Size your shapes with the measurements on the ruler.

If you have a personal die-cut machine such as a Sizzix, cutting letters and shapes from fabrics couldn't be easier. Place one or two sheets of paper underneath your fabric and pull down the handle firmly to cut the die-cut. If you are fusing the shapes, apply the web material to the wrong side of the fabric before cutting.

FUSING

Use a paper-backed fusible web to fuse fabric to other surfaces such as other fabrics, card stock, cardboard or wood. Trace the patterns or draw the desired shape onto the paper side of the fusible web. Trace the patterns to face to the opposite direction they will face on the finished project. Once fused, the patterns will face the correct direction. Cut out each web shape about $1/4$ inch beyond the traced lines. Fuse the web shapes onto the wrong side of the corresponding fabric, following the web manufacturer's instructions. If heated, let the fabric cool. Cut out the shapes with sharp scissors on the drawn lines. Remove the paper backing and position the shapes as desired on the background surface. Fuse the shapes in place, following the manufacturer's instructions.

GLUING

There are many adhesive projects available. Some, like thick crafts glue, are multipurpose and others have very specific uses. Spray adhesives work well when you need to cover a large area with fabric. Lightly spray the surface and smooth the adhesive over the fabric. A glue gun is an indispensable tool for numerous projects but needs to be used with care due to the extremely high temperatures. An alternative to liquid glues or a glue gun is a double-sided adhesive that does not require drying time. Refer to the project instructions for suggestions on adhesives and be sure to follow the manufacturer's directions.

DECOUPAGING

Decoupage fabric onto a variety of surfaces including paper, glass, tin, leather, plastic or wood surfaces. The selected surface should be clean and free of dust. Some surfaces should be sealed or painted before decoupage application. Use a fabric scissors to cut out your fabric shapes. Determine the shape either by a motif printed on the fabric or whatever shape you need to cover the surface. Arrange the shapes on the surface, overlapping them if you like. When you are happy with the arrangement, make a mental note of the positions and remove them from the surface. Lay the shape face down and use a foam brush to completely cover the back with decoupage medium or white glue diluted with water. Work from the center outward on large shapes, brushing the medium on smoothly. Also apply a thin layer of medium on the corresponding area of the surface to be covered. Place the shape medium-side down on the surface. Use a damp cloth to smooth out any wrinkles and to wipe off excess medium. Apply all of your shapes and let the medium dry. Coat the entire top surface of your item with medium, applying as many coats as needed to make the shape edges smooth. Let the medium dry between coats.

SEWING SIMPLE STITCHES

Very few projects in this book require sewing; those that do, call for simple, basic stitches. To work these common stitches, thread an embroidery needle with floss and refer to the following instructions as a guide:

BACKSTITCH—Backstitches are worked in a straight or curved line in a forward and backward motion. Bring the needle up through the fabric at one point and go down with the needle behind that point. Come up in front of the first point and then insert the needle at the original point. Continue in this manner in a line.

OUTLINE OR STEM—The stem stitch is worked in a straight or curved line in a forward and backward motion. This stitch is much the same as the backstitch except the new stitch overlaps half of the last stitch.

RUNNING STITCH—Weave the needle in and out of the fabric to make even stitches on the front of the fabric with same-size spaces between the stitches.

STRAIGHT STITCH—The straight stitch simply comes up at one point and down at the other.

FRENCH KNOT—French knots are tiny knots of thread on the front surface of the fabric. Bring the needle up on the front of the fabric and wrap the thread around the needle, one time for a small knot and multiple times for larger knots. Slide the wraps down to the tip of the needle and insert the needle back into the fabric very close to where it came out. Pull the needle through to the back, holding the wrapped thread tightly around the needle to form the knot.

STIFFENING

You can stiffen fabric with several products. Some of the products require you to shape the fabric first and then spray the stiffener over the fabric. Shape the fabric over any form, such as crumpled aluminum foil. Cover the desired form with plastic wrap and hold the fabric in place with stainless-steel straight pins as needed. Spray as many coats as needed to achieve the desired stiffness, allowing the stiffener to dry between coats. Other products pour and spread over the fabric first, then glue is applied to the wrong side of the fabric before being pressed and shaped onto the final surface.

RIPPING

To tear fabric, use the scissors to make tiny slits at one selvage of the fabric. Space the slits according to how wide you want your strips. Firmly hold the selvage of the fabric above and below a slit and pull to tear the fabric along the crosswise grain. Tear as many strips as needed for the project. Remove any loose threads from the strips. For a different look, remove threads from the strips to fray the edges.

PAINTING

Wash and dry the fabric without fabric softeners or dryer sheets to remove any finishes or sizing. Press the fabric so it is smooth and stretch it taut over a nonporous surface, such as a wax- or plastic-coated board. Use paints specifically manufactured for fabrics or mix acrylic paint with a textile medium. The medium prevents the acrylic paint from bleeding and allows the paint to become permanent when it dries. If using fabric paints, follow the manufacturer's instructions.

There are several ways to apply designs onto fabric. Purchase an iron-on transfer or make your own with iron-on transfer pens. Trace the design on tracing paper, then flip over the tracing and retrace with a heat transfer pen. Iron the design onto the fabric. Another method is to freehand draw directly onto the fabric with an erasable fabric marker. Apply paint with a synthetic or nylon fabric brush.

Whatever method you choose to apply paint, it is usually suggested that you heat-set the paint. Refer to the fabric-paint or textile-medium manufacturer's instructions for advice on heat-setting and fabric care.

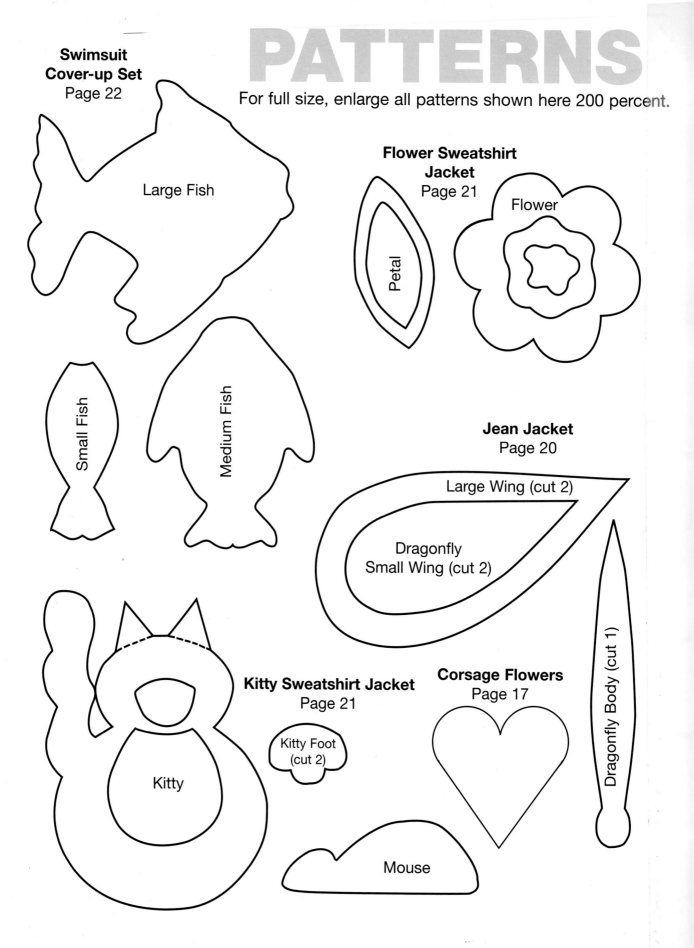

PATTERNS

For full size, enlarge all patterns shown here 200 percent.

Swimsuit Cover-up Set
Page 22

Large Fish

Small Fish

Medium Fish

Flower Sweatshirt Jacket
Page 21

Petal

Flower

Jean Jacket
Page 20

Large Wing (cut 2)

Dragonfly Small Wing (cut 2)

Dragonfly Body (cut 1)

Kitty Sweatshirt Jacket
Page 21

Kitty

Kitty Foot (cut 2)

Corsage Flowers
Page 17

Mouse